© 2017 Holmes, Investments and Holdings, LLC.
All Rights Reserved
No part of this publication may be reproduced, stored in a retrieval system, or transmitted, in any form or by any means, electronic, mechanical, photocopying, recording, or otherwise, without the written permission of the author.
This book is a work of fiction. Places, events, and situations in this book are purely fictional and any resemblance to actual persons, living or dead, is coincidental.
Printed in the United States of America

ISBN: 978-0-9992369-8-7

# JOHNNY SKIP 2

The Amazing Adventures of Johnny Skip 2 in Australia

## COLORING BOOK

By Quentin Holmes

Hi, my name is Johnny but all my friends call me Johnny Skip 2. That's because I skip all over the world. Come along with me and you can skip too.

We can use my little device; I call it The Amazing, Instant-Travel-Skip 2. It's fifty percent magic and fifty percent science. But altogether, it's one hundred percent cool!

Collecting little things is what I love to do. Do you like collecting little things too?

I have little bitty books, baskets and bags. I collect mini-toy pugs and multi-colored mugs.

Although my best friend is little and rounder, he's an eager brown beagle whose first name is Grounder.

Our travel gear is ready, so we're off on another journey. There's no time to waste. Come on now, let's hurry! Will you travel with us? We could really use your help. Australia is amazing; come see it for yourself!

The Amazing, Instant-Travel-Skip 2 buzzes when you press the button 'begin.' It pauses for a moment and pulls us all in. Off we go quickly and travel so swiftly.

The Amazing, Instant-Travel-Skip 2 is quite fantastic and fast, it makes all of our trips a tremendous blast; and in a blink we land in a field with tall rocks and pale grass.

Welcome to Australia, the place where they say G'day! To fit in with the locals, we've got to speak their way. It never means we're leaving; it's just like saying 'hey!' Now say it like a true Aussie, instead of hello we say... G'day!

Now let's head out to the outback for a special kind of fruit. They're called muntrie berries and they taste like smoky apples do.

If we look around very carefully, we're bound to find some clues. Grounder will lead the way, as we head out on the move.

Wait a minute! Look over there. Do you see that hand waving? Let's go over there behind those trees to see what she is saying.

It's a lady Kangaroo; what are we supposed to say? Do we say hello Mrs. Kangaroo? No, that's right, we say G'day! She says, "G'day to you too mates; I don't want to seem rude, but my little joey is missing and I don't know what to do!"

"Oh my goodness, oh my gracious, I'm so very confused! Could you help me out, mates? I'd appreciate anything you can do." These worried words are from a mama kangaroo. How is it we can tell? A 'joey' is simply a baby kangaroo.

Do you think we should help her out? Is there something we can do? I've got an idea; we'll find her little joey while looking for our fruit!

Mrs. Kangaroo smiles and says, "No gift could be kinder. My joey's name is Rachida. Please tell me if you find her!"

We tell her hooroo for now. Please let me tell you why. The word hooroo is Aussie; it means, for now goodbye.

You check around front while I check around back.
Keep your eyes open for baby kangaroo tracks.
We are hot upon the trail; let's see where these tracks go.

They go past the trees and down the road. We're headed through the bush, and its many miles wide. Bush is just the word that means Australian countryside.

As we take a look around, there are plenty of things to find. There are many plants and fruits, and nuts, and animals of all kinds. Like kangaroos and cockatoos, dingoes, crocs and bandicoots.

There are even birds too big to hide. They're called Emu's but they don't fly. But let's get back to our search; I feel like suddenly we're getting very close.

If we look a little harder, a clue could be under our nose. Just as I begin to say it, what is it that we find? A patch full of muntrie berries with a joey hiding inside!

Excuse me little joey! Is your name Rachida? She looks up with a smile and says, "Yes, it is, nice to meet ya!"

Please come along with us, we need to move quick in a hurry. Your mom is looking for you and she's been very worried.

Rachida says, "thank you kind mates, it's been very scary. As a way of saying thanks, please take some of these berries."

We return to Mrs. Kangaroo and she thanks us through and through. And now it's time to say goodbye, or as the Aussie's say hooroo!

We really saved the day, Grounder, me, and you too! Come along with us on our next adventure and we'll travel someplace new.

We can go anyplace, no matter where you choose. Just remember your friend Johnny and The Amazing Instant-Travel Skip 2!

www.ingramcontent.com/pod-product-compliance
Lightning Source LLC
Chambersburg PA
CBHW060458300426
44113CB00016B/2640